The Ultimate Guide to Blogging

What To Write About, How to Promote Your Blog, & How to Make Money Blogging

Mike Fishbein

www.stpcollege.com

Table of Contents

Introduction

Blogging can be tremendously valuable to both individuals and businesses. The benefits of blogging include business marketing, personal and professional development, business networking, making money online, and more. There has never been a better time to start a blog! Digital marketing is a new frontier and blogging is at the forefront.

The Ultimate Guide to Blogging covers everything you need to know about starting a blog, growing and promoting your blog, making money blogging, and more. Specific topics covered in this book include:

How to Market Your Business by Blogging
How to Promote Your Blog
How to Increase Blog Traffic
What to Blog About
Blog Topics and Blog Post Ideas
How to Make Money Blogging
How to Start a Blog
Hot to Make a Blog
How to Force Yourself to Start Blogging
...and more!

What is a Blog? A blog is website containing written "posts" or articles. Blogs are like miniature media companies. They can be on any on topic the author desires.

Blogging is often used as a form of content marketing. Blog topics can range from personal to professional and everything in between. The Ultimate Guide to Blogging covers content marketing strategy, blog ideas, and more.

Can you make money blogging? Yes. Ways to make money blogging include affiliate marketing, selling ebooks, premium content, additional products and services, and more. This book covers how to make money with a blog.

Blogging has been tremendously beneficial to me professionally, personally, and financially, so I'm very excited to be sharing what I've learned with you. The contents of this book has been developed in response to questions people have asked me about blogging, It addresses the challenges that I, and many others, have faced in starting and growing a blog. I recommend blogging to almost everyone I meet. With this book, I can now do more than just recommend, I can provide all of my best advice.

About the Author

Mike Fishbein is an entrepreneur in New York City, author of multiple books on entrepreneurship, and has advised both startups and fortune 500 companies on customer development and new product innovation.

Mike is the Founder of stpcollege.com, an education technology company in New York City. With over 2,000 enrolled students, stpcollege.com's online courses help entrepreneurs start and grow their companies.

Prior to stpcollege.com, Mike was a founding team member of Casual Corp, a venture studio and corporate innovation firm founded by an accomplished serial entrepreneur. While at Casual Corp, Mike served as a lead product manager in launching three new consumer technology products. In addition, Mike advised some of the world's largest companies on new product innovation.

Mike's expertise lies in customer development, Lean product strategy, and customer acquisition. His writings on startup marketing and strategy have been published in Huffington Post, Entrepreneur, and more.

Mike has been starting companies since he was a teenager and serves as a resource and advisor to startups in New York City in abroad. You can learn more about Mike via his personal blog, mfishbein.com.

Mike is the author of four other books:

1. "Customer Development for Entrepreneurs: How to Test Startup Ideas and Build Products People Love"

2. "Business Networking: How to Build an Awesome Professional Network"

3. "Do More, Better, Faster & Happier: How to Boost Energy for Happiness and Productivity"

4. "Growth Hacking with Content Marketing: How to Increase Website Traffic"

To Learn more about marketing, growth hacking, social media marketing, and how to increase website traffic, check out Startup College at stpcollege.com

Why You Should be Blogging

Blogging can be incredibly valuable to a variety of people and for a variety of reasons. Below are the primary benefits to blogging. Benefits for businesses and entrepreneurs will be discussed in a future chapter. At the end of this chapter, I will describe all the different types of people that can benefit from blogging, how they can benefit, and what blogging strategies they could initiate to receive those benefits.

1. Attract an Audience

Blogging enables you to reach the billions of people that use the Internet every day. Blogging can help you promote yourself or your business. Blogging works as a method for attracting an audience because it provides something of value to them.

What would you rather click on, a page titled "How to Make Money Blogging," or a page titled "Buy My Consulting Services"? By creating a blog that is of value, you can attract an audience and eventually convert them to customers, partners, friends, or otherwise.

2. Establishes Authority

Having a blog and writing about important topics that are relevant to your audience establishes yourself as an authority in the space. It enhances your professional image. A blog is to professionals in the 2000s what a business card was in the 1990s. Blogs are the new business cards.

3. Build Rapport, Engagement and Relationships

One potential goal of a blog is to generate traffic, or visitors, and to convert that traffic into customers, users, or otherwise. Blogging can convert traffic into leads and leads into customers.

Blogging can "warm up" your cold calls and traffic from other sources. If someone sees your facebook ad, or receives your cold call, they may be more receptive if they've read your blog and received value from it.

4. Create Opportunities

Blogging can lead to other business/traffic generating opportunities. Such as speaking engagements or press. I've had people contact me to speak at conferences and events based on my blog posts. I was also offered to take over a LinkedIn group in my space because I had been posting my blog posts there. Blogging enables anyone with something interesting or valuable to say to be identified as an expert.

5. Organize Your Thoughts and Learn

Blogging forces you to teach yourself what you don't know and to articulate what you do know. When you begin writing a given post, you are forced to organize your thoughts. If there are any gaps in the topic that you are writing about, you will have to learn about it. Writing out and articulating your thoughts is a great way to formalize something you've learned and help "internalize" it. After you have written something you may become much more familiar with the topic.

6. Tell Your Story

Blogging enables you to be your own media company. You can tell your story the way you want to tell it without being dependent on journalists. Sometimes an editor, journalist, or media company may have incorrect information and/or present it in a negative light.

When you are writing about a topic of your own interest, you can decide how to portray a story, what information to include, and what information to exclude. This also allow you to ensure that all information included in the blog is factual.

7. Meet New People

The audience you attract through blogging doesn't have to just be your "audience." They can become your friends, colleagues, partners, or important members of your professional network. I've had many people reach out to me directly after reading my blog. Some of those people have become friends or good business contacts.

8. Stand Out From the Crowd

According to the "1% rule," only 1% of Internet users actively create new content, while the other 99% of the participants view it. By blogging, you instantly separate yourself from the 99% of people that don't blog. In an increasingly competitive economy, standing out is essential.

9. Validate Expertise

Blogs are the new resumes. Blogging about a topic you would like to be viewed as an expert in, can illustrate to readers, employers, and your network, that you are are skilled and knowledgeable.

10. Make Money

If you have a blog with a lot of viewers, there may be significant income potential. In today's economy, where there is much uncertainty and jobs are being automated and outsourced, being diversified and having additional sources of income can be tremendously beneficial.

If you want to quit your job, a blog could be a great business. If you lost your job and are worried about finding a new one, blogging can be a great way to earn income. If you are working a job that doesn't pay as much as you'd like, or if you would simply like to earn more money (who doesn't?), blogging can make for a great side income.

Income generated from blogging can also be "passive," meaning it can be automated and is not directly correlated to the amount of time you put in to it. I will cover the topic of monetizing a blog in the chapter "How to Make Money Blogging."

Who Should be Blogging

Below section covers the types of people that can benefit most from blogging, why they will benefit, and what blogging strategies they can use to receive these benefits.

Who: Entrepreneurs, marketers, small businesses, and startups
Why: Drive traffic to your website; engage and build rapport with your audience
Strategy: Write and distribute blog posts that are valuable to your target audience.

Who: Job Seekers
Why: Display your expertise
Strategy: Write a "case study" about an accomplishment from a past job; write a "how to" about a skills needed for a position you are seeking.

Who: Unemployed
Why: Make money; avoid boredom; attract potential employers

Strategy: Write about topics you enjoy, display expertise in areas you would like to be employed in, and/or find a profitable niche to fill.

Who: Students
Why: Internalize your learnings and organize your thoughts
Strategy: Write a blog post summarizing every class you attend, chapter you read, etc.

Who: Teachers
How: Organize your thoughts on a topic before teaching it verbally
Strategy: Before every lecture you give, outline for the topic in the form of a blog post.

Blogging 101

The following chapter includes some basic blogging tips and advice for beginners.

What is a blog?

A blog is a website containing written "posts." It is often used by business as a form of content marketing. There is an entire section on content marketing is later in this book. Blogging is also done for fun. Blogs can be on any topic imaginable.

What You Need to Know About Blogging

1. There are Many Benefits of Blogging

The benefits of blogging are discussed in detail in the previous chapter. To quickly recap, the benefits of blogging include meeting new people, personal and professional development, organizing your thoughts, reaching a new audience, and making money.

2. Everyone Should Blog

Almost everyone in the world can benefit in one or more ways from blogging. I recommend blogging to almost everyone I meet. You don't have to be an "expert" or have something completely unique to write about in order to benefit from blogging.

3. Blogging Takes Time

The benefits of blogging don't always come right away. It usually takes time to find your voice and build an audience. Depending on your writing speed, it may even take a long time to write a blog post.

4. You Can Make Money from a Blog

In today's economy, it seems like everyone could use a little extra cash. There are several ways to make money from blogging that I will discuss in detail in the chapter titled "How to Make Money Blogging."

5. It's Easy to Start a Blog

You don't need any technical ability, programming skills, or computer science skills to start a blog. Technology companies such as WordPress and Tumblr make it incredibly easy for anyone to start a blog. You can start a basic blog for free. Premium features, such as a personal domain name, usually don't cost much.

6. There are Many Reason to Blog

Blogging can be done for fun, for profit, for promotion, or otherwise. Not all blogs are used for content marketing or business purposes.

7. Blogs Come in Different Shapes and Sizes

Blogs can be personal or professional. They can include text, video, and/or pictures. They can be on WordPress, Quora, Tumblr, and more. Blogs can be on any topic you choose. Who you are, why you are blogging, and the results you desire should determine the shape and size of your blog.

8. Blogs Should Have Educational or Entertainment Value

One of the core principles of content marketing is that content should deliver value to your target audience. If you're using blogging as a form of content marketing, your blog, and the posts you write, should deliver value to your target audience.

Value generally comes in two forms: educational value and entertainment value. Educational value helps the audience learn something. "How to" posts generally have educational value. Entertainment value brings the audience fun or enjoyment. Photo blogs generally have more entertainment value than educational value to most audiences.

9. If You're Serious About Blogging...

If you would eventually like to monetize your blog, and/or if you want to attract a large audience, use WordPress and learn about search engine optimization. I will explain Wordpress and the different blogging platforms later in this book. I will also provide an introduction to search engine optimization.

6 Myths About Blogging

Below are some of the most common misconceptions I hear about blogging.

1. It's Easy

Because it's so easy to make and launch a blog, people think it's easy to grow and maintain a blog. There are many challenges associated with blogging and growing an audience. Challenges include identifying topics to write about on a regular basis, and attracting a large audience.

2. It's a Get Rich Quick Scheme

While blogging can be quite lucrative, it doesn't happen overnight for most. It takes time. If it was easy, everyone would be doing it, and it would therefore be more competitive and less profitable. Not all blogs make money. Some blogs only make small amounts of money. Results can vary; there is no such thing as a free lunch.

3. There's No Benefit to Having a Blog Unless a Lot of People Read It

There are so many benefits to blogging, having an audience is certainly one of them, but is not the only one. Blogging helps you organize your thoughts and can be therapeutic to many people. Many people prefer smaller, focused, higher quality, audiences to generate more value.

If the blog reaches potential employers, customers or people in your network, it has generated value. If just one potential employer reads your blog, that may be all you need to land a job. If just one potential customer reads your blog, that is better than not having any customers read your blog.

4. Every Business Should Blog

I do think almost every business could benefit from blogging in one way or another. Almost every major demographic of people in developed countries actively use the Internet. However, some don't use the Internet or consume blog content as much as others. For businesses that serve customers who are less active on the Internet or consume blog content less actively, a blog might not be the most lucrative marketing channel.

5. You Need to Be Unique

"I don't have anything to write about" is one of the most common aversions to blogging that I hear. Everyone has unique experiences or knowledge. You don't even need to write about anything extremely unique in order to get value from blogging. In fact, you can still benefit from writing a blog, even if no one reads it.

It's not always the best or most unique blog that gets read. Sometimes it's the blog that people find first that gets read. Sometimes people like to read multiple blogs on the same topic, in the same way they read several books or watch more than one movie on the same topic.

6. You Need to Be an Expert

I've had many people tell me they believe that since they're not at the top of their field that they should avoid blogging. Even if you have "intermediate level" knowledge of a given topic, someone who has "beginner level" or no knowledge of a topic may get a tremendous amount of value from reading what you know. In addition, blogging can make you appear to be more of an expert than you actually are!

Content Marketing 101

Traditional marketing and advertising is broken. Traditional advertising methods like billboards, TV and radio advertising, paper mail advertising, and cold calling are expensive, hard to measure, inefficiently targeted, and often ineffective. How many times do you switch to a different TV channel when a commercial is running? You know an industry is in trouble when people are actively paying to get it out of their face.

People don't get sold anymore, they buy. Annoying people is not a good way to get them to buy something! Enter content marketing, a more efficient and effective way to attract, engage, and acquire customers.

Even though blogging is for everyone, much of this book is about using a blog as content marketing for a business, I wanted to cover the basics of content marketing before I dive in to the meat of this book. To learn more about content marketing, check out "Growth Hacking with Content Marketing" at mfishbein.com/contentmarketing.

What is Content Marketing?

Definition

What exactly is content marketing? You've probably heard the term but many misunderstand what it actually is. I'm going to give you a rather "dense" definition of content marketing and then I'll break down each component of it.

Content marketing is a strategy for attracting, engaging and acquiring customers. It entails creating and/or curating relevant and valuable content.

What does that actually mean? Keep reading...

2 Forms of Value

Per the above definition, content must be valuable to the target audience. What does it mean to be valuable? Value, as it pertains to content marketing, comes in two primary forms:

a. Entertainment Value

The audience finds the content funny, interesting, or otherwise entertaining. The best example of content marketing that has entertainment value is Dollar Shave Club's YouTube video that now has over 13 million views.

People watched it, even multiple times, and shared it, because they enjoyed watching it. The fact that it's an advertisement is an afterthought. In addition, it improves Dollar Shave Club's brand by making them look "cool."

b. Educational Value

The audience finds the content helpful. It answers their questions or gives them information that they can use to solve their problems or in some way improve themselves.

The best example of content marketing that has educational value is Moz's beginner's guide to SEO. It's become like the bible on beginning SEO. It is the "go to" source for anyone that wants to learn SEO.

The fact that Moz did it to attract it's target audience, marketers, is not even recognized at first glance. In addition, it improves Moz's brand by displaying their expertise, and building a perception of being helpful.

9 Ways Content Marketing Can Grow Your Business

Content marketing can help companies with several aspects of the customer acquisition funnel. I've grouped them into three buckets:

a. Attract

"People" see you, find you and/or become aware that you exist. They become your "audience."

b. Engage

Your "audience" gets to know you and starts to like you. You build a relationship with your audience. They become "potential customers."

c. Acquire

"Potential customers" pay for your product or service, and become "customers."

Below are nine ways content marketing can help companies attract people, engage with them, and convert them into customers.

1. Establishes Authority

Producing content that displays expertise instantly improves the perception of the author's authority on the topic. A book is probably the form of content that improves authority the most, but several other forms, including a blog, can help. Improving your image of authority should improve conversion rates from "people" to "customers."

Who do you think people are more likely to hire to do, say marketing -- someone off the street, or someone who's written a book on marketing?

2. Builds Relationships

Content marketing increases engagement, rapport and trust with your audience.

When a customer sees your billboard, they see it for a few seconds and then probably forget about it. When someone reads your blog, they're on your website, listening to what you're saying, and potentially for extended periods of time. This enables them to get to know you. I've met people who had been following my blog and as a result know a lot about me and feel like they know me, even though we haven't met in person.

People like to do business with organizations and individuals they know, like, and trust.

An extreme example of content that builds rapport is James Altucher's blog. James shares his deepest emotions and personal stories. Most of us don't have to go that far to build rapport with your audience.

Simply sharing your opinions on industry topics or adding some character to your writing can help. Don't be afraid to take a controversial stance if appropriate or use less than perfect grammar if it adds character. Who do you think people would rather hire - someone off the street, or a friend?

3. Reach a Wider Audience

People don't always search for a specific product or service, they often look for information or solutions to problems. For example, per Google Keyword Planner, "productivity consultant" gets just 70 average monthly searches, while "how to be more productive" gets 1,300. Keyword searches can be used as a proxy for people's actual interests and buying behaviors.

Content marketing can enable you to reach an audience beyond what can be reached by cold calling or advertising. They could also find you if one of their Facebook friends shares a piece of your content.

People post about specific products far less than they share content that's entertaining or educational. After building rapport, establishing yourself as an expert, and adding value, a customer may be more interested in your product or service.

4. Improves Search Engine Optimization

A company's search ranking is driven by two primary categories: onsite and offsite. Content marketing helps with both. Onsite factors are the aspects of a given web page that influence search engine ranking. Offsite factors influence search ranking based on aspects outside of your site.

Content marketing helps with onsite primarily by making your site more frequently updated. Google prefers sites with recently updated content. If you are actively creating new content, Google will better index you.

Content marketing helps with offsite SEO by improving your chances of being linked to. Google interprets someone else linking to you as a sign that your site is of value. People are far more likely to link to a valuable blog post you wrote than simply your sales page.

Better search ranking means more traffic. Ranking higher on a search engine like google means people are more likely to find you. You can bring a large number to the "attract" bucket as described above.

If none of that makes sense, don't worry, there is a chapter later in this book on SEO.

5. Leads to Sales

At the end of the day sales are what you really want - right? After all, you are running a business, not a charity. Content marketing can directly help with that. As discussed above, a person will click through to a site that has perceived value, versus a sales page. However, viewing the content will lead the viewer to your "sales page."

This could play itself out in many different ways, but let me give you two quick examples. First example: viewer searches for a topic you've been blogging about...finds your blog post...signs up for your email newsletter...reads your emails each week, and thinks you're awesome…two months later when you send out an email about your new product launch they buy because they've "known" you for two months and know that you're "legit."

Second example: a person searches iTunes for a podcast related to their interest...finds you and listens to one...you mention one of your products and tell listeners where they can find it...listener finds it and becomes a customer.

Who would you rather hire, someone you've known for two seconds or someone you've known for two months?

6. People Share It

When people share your content, you get more exposure. Exposure leads to traffic. This is the "attract" bucket per above. Sharing also improves your brand. If people see their friends talking about you they may think more highly of you. This is the "engage" bucket per above.

People are more likely to share content they find valuable than your sales page.

How do you get most of your restaurant, movie, product, etc. recommendations? Word of mouth? A lot of people rely on their friends for recommendations.

7. Free or Cheap

Most forms of content marketing don't cost much to produce. Blogging, for example, costs almost nothing. All you need is a computer and an Internet connection, which you probably already have.

It does however take time. If you get into more advanced content production, such as research reports, or even podcasts, you may need some special equipment that costs money.

However, many forms of content marketing have almost no up-front costs, which make it great for startups, self-published authors, or anyone on a budget.

Would you rather pay for customers or get them for free?

8. Targeted

With content marketing, you can be more sure you're reaching your target audience then, for example, billboards or TV ads. Yes, you can get demographic data on who drives on the road, who watches the show, etc. But with content you can be even more precise.

For example, you can use Google's keyword planner to get data on the number of times a given search term is being made and who is actually making the searches. You can write blog posts to to match those terms. Or you can write a post like "marketing for startups" to be sure your audience knows it's for them.

If you're selling a product for Moms, would you rather reach ten random people or ten mothers of three year olds?

9. Collect Email Addresses

People are very attentive to their inboxes. As a marketer, you want to be where their attention is. You don't need to pay for a list if you're doing content marketing. Offer something of value in exchange for signing up for your email newsletter, to increase your email signups. It could be as simple as receiving your blog posts by email. Offering an ebook or white paper is even better. What percentage of Tweets on your Twitter stream do you read? What percentage of your emails do you read?

10 Types of Content to Produce to Get Results

Content can come in many shapes and sizes. Most people think of blogs when they think of content marketing. Blogging is a great one, and is of course the focus of this book, however there are many, many formats in which you can produce content for marketing.

Below are several formats/platforms to produce content on. Each of these platforms has slightly different user base demographics, enabling you to reach wider audiences.

1. Video courses on Udemy

2. Answers on Quora

3. Blog posts

4. Curated content as an email newsletter

5. Podcasts

6. Presentations on SlideShare

7. Videos on YouTube

8. Self-published books on Amazon

9. Microcontent on social networks - tweets, status updates, Instagram photos, etc.

10. Public speaking, webinars, workshops, etc.

Each of these formats can deliver educational and/or entertainment value, and can therefore help attract, engage, and acquire customers.

2 Excellent Pieces of Content Marketing Advice

1. Create content that's valuable to your audience! If you do that, people will find you, share you, engage with you, return to you, etc. Put in the extra time and effort to make sure your content is valuable to your target audience.

2. Capture your audience. Don't just produce content for the sake of producing content. Produce it to get results. Engage with the people who find your content and turn them into customers. I'll talk about how to do that later in the book.

To learn more about content marketing, check out "Growth Hacking with Content Marketing: How to Increase Website Traffic" at mfishbein.com/contentmarketing.

How to Use a Blog to Market Your Business

Blogging can be an amazing source of free traffic. For some companies/products it's their most profitable, high volume, and sustainable marketing channel. Blogging has benefits to business beyond traffic as well. It can be used to attract, engage, and acquire customers.

This chapter covers 1) what makes blogging such a great source of traffic, 2) how to use blogging to increase website traffic, 3) how to use blogging to convert traffic into customers...and more.

Why Blog: 7 Reasons Blogging is a Great Source of Traffic for Business

1. Establishes Authority

Having a blog and writing about important topics that are relevant to your audience establishes you as an authority. Customers and potential customers may therefore have a better perception of you. A better perception can increase referrals, social shares, and or improve the rate of conversion from "engage" to "acquire."

2. Customers Like Blogs

It's no secret that people like reading articles and blog posts and often search for them. Give your customers what they want! Providing value to customers is the very core of what makes companies work.

3. Converts Traffic Into Customers

The reason you want traffic is probably not just for the sake of traffic, but to convert that traffic into customers or users. Blogging can convert traffic into leads and leads into customers. More on that later in this chapter.

4. Low Cost

Blogging takes time, but not a lot of money. If you're a startup, self-published author, or freelance consultant, free traffic is a must. But who doesn't like free traffic?

5. Sustainable

Blogging can be a sustainable long-term marketing channel. Facebook ads and Tweets come and go, but your blog posts will always be indexed by Google. The content you produce on different platforms, such as SlideShare, will always be searchable.

6. Builds Rapport

After someone finds your site, they can get to know you better if they read your blog. This is the "engage" bucket as described previously. Some products or services require deep engagement before a customer will "convert." Without a blog, there might not be an opportunity to engage with the potential customer, and could therefore reduce the number of customers.

As discussed previously, blogging can also "warm up" your cold calls and traffic from other sources. If someone sees your facebook ad, or receives your cold call, they may be more receptive if they've read your blog and received value from it.

7. Creates Opportunities

Blogging can lead to other business/traffic generating opportunities. Such as speaking engagements or press. I've had people reach out to me asking me to speak at conferences and events citing my blog posts. I was also offered to take over a LinkedIn group in my space because I had been posting my blog posts there.

These "secondary" opportunities can be great opportunities to attract potential customers.

In addition to customers, you can also attract other professional contacts who may be able to help your business. Potential partners, hires, affiliates, journalists, etc. might find you through your blog.

2 Ways Blogging Can Drive Traffic to Your Website

1. Search

Assuming you've chosen to do so, you blog posts will be indexed by Google. Therefore, you increase the likelihood of people finding you through search. If your text matches the keywords people are searching for, you increase your chances even more.

Remember, people don't always search for product names, or even product categories, they search for answers to their questions or solutions to their problems. Blogging is a great way to be that solution.

In addition, every blog post you write, is another indexed page on your website. It's one more cue to Google and

other search engines that your website is active.
Google likes active websites.

2. Social Shares

People like to share content they think their audience
will find valuable. People won't always tweet about a
product, but they might tweet a blog post about
"Pinterest marketing for startups" if they found it
interesting.

Blogging increases your chance of being shared. Your
posts could also be linked to by other bloggers which
will boost your SEO.

8 Ways to Get More Traffic From Blogging

1. Be the answer to your customers' search queries

Do some keyword research to determine what people
are searching for. Create content that matches it.

2. Write posts about 500 to 1,250 words in length

Both customers and Google like content in that range. If it's any shorter, it probably won't be very valuable. If it's too long, people might get bored.

3. Write highly entertaining, valuable, and/or educational blog posts

Know your audience and what they want. If you don't know, ask them. Write epic content that people will want to bookmark, share and link to. Getting shared and linked to can lead to massive results! You can read more about how to generate blog topic ideas later in this book.

4. Add images to increase engagement

Blog posts with images tend to stand out more in Facebook, Twitter, etc. They're also appealing to the eyes of viewers once they're on the page.

5. Share your blog posts on your social channels and in relevant social networks

Figure out who your target customer is and where they hang out online; use those sites as distribution channels. For example, If you're marketing to businesses or professionals, definitely share on LinkedIn. If you're marketing to developers or entrepreneurs, share on Hacker News. You can read more about how to distribute your blog posts and promote your blog later in this book.

6. Add some personality

Make sure your posts are informative and/or educational, but don't be afraid to add some color. It builds rapport and adds a human element, which people like. As I've mentioned, the blogger who I think does this best is James Altucher. He shares his stories, opinions and beliefs...and basically bleeds his emotions onto the page.

7. Write consistently

You don't have to blog every day, but try to at least blog once per week so that when people return to your site, they will have something new to read. It will also keep you in the habit of blogging. Blogging consistently will keep you on top of your network's mind and remind them that they should be returning to your site regularly.

8. Use WordPress

WordPress is a blogging platform that makes it really easy to improve SEO. It's easy to edit link structures, meta descriptions etc. Yoast, and other WordPress plugins make it easier to improve SEO. This book has a chapter dedicated to comparing the different blogging platforms.

2 Blogging Tactics to Convert Traffic into Customers

Not only is blogging a great source of traffic, it can help you convert traffic into leads, and leads into customers. Here are a few tactics you can use to increase your conversions.

1. Create a mailing list

Get people to subscribe to your mailing list. Someone might land on your site, not buy, and then browse away and forget about you. But if they like your blog content they might subscribe to your mailing list. You will then be able to re-engage them after sending out future blog posts. Later in this book, you can read about how to get people to sign up for your mailing list.

2. Send blog posts instead of more nagging sales emails

If you have a lead that you're trying to push through the pipeline to a customer, your blog content gives you great ammunition. Instead of simply writing a nagging sales email, include a blog post, or send it on it's own if it's relevant to them. They will appreciate the value you're providing them (assuming the blog post is good). And it will display your expertise in the space (again, assuming the post is good).

How to Create a Blog

You don't need any technical abilities to create a blog. It's easy and cheap or free to launch a fully functional blog. The following chapter describes the pros and cons of several different blogging platforms. Spoiler alert: I recommend Wordpress. Especially if you want to attract a wide audience, and/or monetize your blog.

Blogging Platforms

What's the best blogging platform? There are several blogging platforms. They each have different strengths and weaknesses and serve slightly different customers. I don't think there is one blogging platform that every single blogger should use. The blogging platform that you should choose is dependent on your goals as a blogger.

Below is a brief description of the most popular blogging platforms. I originally started blogging on Tumblr and later switched to WordPress. Switching from Tumblr to WordPress was a bit of a pain, so I recommend choosing your platform carefully. I also do some blogging on Quora.

My my personal blog (mfishbein.com) is on WordPress. I also use Wordpress, for my company, stpcollege.com's blog. I use Quora mostly for "side projects."

1. Tumblr

What is Tumblr?

Tumblr is a microblogging platform and social networking site. It was started in New York and was acquired by Yahoo! for over $1 billion in 2013. You can find Tumblr at http://snip.ly/bVw.

Benefits of Tumblr

The benefits of Tumblr include it's ease of use, slick interface, and community. Tumblr is a network. The network effect makes it easier for others to find your blog. In addition, some of the network is very active with commenting and re-blogging.

Who Should Use Tumblr?

Tumblr is best for short form content, and for content within certain niches. Tumblr has a more active user base in niches like art and photography. If you are writing short-form content or want to reach the kinds of audiences that are active on Tumblr, I would recommend using Tumblr. I would recommend creating a free account and browsing other blogs before committing to it.

2. WordPress

What is WordPress?

WordPress is a free and open source blogging tool and content management system. According to Wikipedia, WordPress is used by 22% of the top 10 million websites as of August 2013 and is the most popular blogging system in use on the web.

Benefits of WordPress

WordPress is great because it allows you to create a blog, and other types of websites, very quickly, easily, and cheaply. You do not need any coding abilities. All you have to do is sign up.

WordPress makes it easy to search engine optimize your site and blog posts. In addition, there is a great network of plugin and theme developers.

WordPress "plug ins" offer custom functions and features enabling users to tailor their sites to their specific needs. These plugins include Mailchimp integration, Disqus commenting, SEO enhancers, social share buttons, and more. I describe my favorite plug ins below.

Wordpress "themes" allow users to change the look and functionality of a WordPress site without altering the code of the site. Many come available within WordPress automatically. There are also many that are available for free or for a small price. Searching google "for WordPress Themes" will give you a large volume of resources.

Who Should Use WordPress?

If your goal is to build a large audience, and/or monetize your blog, I recommend WordPress. If you plan to write long form blog posts, I recommend WordPress.

WordPress Plugins

There are some amazing WordPress plugins that are available for free that make blogging on WordPress easier and more effective. Below are my favorite WordPress plugins:

a. Mailchimp:

As I mention in this book, building a mailing list is a great way to build engagement with readers. Mailchimp is my preferred email marketing app. The Mailchimp WordPress plugin enables you to embed an email sign up form on your blog.

b. Pretty Link:

According to the the plug in's developer, Pretty Link enables you to "Shrink, track and share any URL on the Internet from your WordPress website. Unlike other link shrinking services like tinyurl, budurl, and bit.ly, this plugin allows you to create short links coming from your own domain!"

Pretty Link is great for masking affiliate links and for verbally pointing people to a certain page. For example, if you are doing a Podcast or public speaking gig, you wouldn't want to point people to a really long complicated web address, or even tell them where to search. Make it as easy as possible for people by creating a an easy to pronounce and read address. You can find Pretty Link at http://snip.ly/ccb.

c. Digg Digg

This plug in makes it easy for your readers to share your posts on their social networks. Digg Digg displays share buttons for each social network. The buttons "float" as the user scrolls up and down the screen.

Getting social shares is a great way to promote your blog. This plug in is the best looking and functioning share plug in I've seen.

d. Google Analytics:

According to it's developer, "This plugin makes it simple to add Google Analytics to your WordPress blog, adding lots of features, eg. custom variables and automatic clickout and download tracking." Google Analytics is one of the most essential tools for anyone who is serious about blogging. You can learn more about it on the chapter on blogging tools.

e. WordPress SEO:

This plug in makes it easier to search engine optimize each of your blog posts. It's one of the most popular WordPress plugins and is extremely easy to use.

3. Quora Blogs

What is Quora?

Quora is a question and answer site that includes a blogging function. If you have a Quora account, you can create a blog within a few clicks. Creating a Quora account only takes a few minutes and is free.

Benefits of Blogging on Quora

a. Built in SEO:

Quora already has a decent search ranking. By creating a site with a Quora domain, your value will therefore have a headstart on search ranking. A blog post on Quora is more likely to rank higher than an equivalent post on a new domain.

b. Built in audience:

When you blog on Quora, you select the topics of the blog post. Users on Quora can follow topics they choose. If a user is following the topic of your blog post, it may appear in their "news feed."

c. Searchable on Quora:

Quora has a lot of active users. Many people use Quora to get answers to their own questions. Quora has a search functionality that allows people to enter search terms or questions they have. By having a blog on Quora, your blog will appear in the search results if it's relevant to the keywords the searcher used.

d. Sharability:

Quora gives readers the option to "upvote" blog posts made on Quora blogs. When a user upvotes a post it appears in the "news feed" of anyone who is following that user.

e. Quora credits:

When your posts on Quora get upvoted, you receive "credits." People upvote posts that they think are high quality. Credits can be used to promote posts to Quora users. Promoting on Quora works similar to promoted tweets on Twitter, except it's free. Earning Quora credits can be quite valuable.

Who Should Blog on Quora?

There are a few factors to consider when deciding whether or not to blog on Quora:

a. Audience - Certain demographics of people are more active on Quora than others. Browse questions and topics within your niche to see how active the community is. If your target audience is active on Quora, starting a blog on Quora could be a great way to attract them.

b. Quick - If you want to reach an audience quickly, Quora might be a better option than something like WordPress. However, WordPress may enable you to get more traffic in the long term.

c. Design - Quora does not give you much control over the design of your blog. If you don't care much about your design, or if you like Quora's design, Quora is an excellent option.

d. Easy - A benefit of Quora's reduced customizability and functionality, is that Quora blogs are extremely easy to use. Perhaps easier to use than any other blogging platform. You can create a blog and publish your first post in under ten clicks of the mouse.

4. Medium

What is Medium?

Medium is a blogging platform that positions itself like an "online magazine." It was started by co-founders of the microcontent social network, Twitter. Anyone can blog on Medium for free and it is very easy to start a blog on Medium.

Benefits of Medium

a. Design - Medium has a very slick interface that comes included with Medium. You do not have to design or customize a Medium blog the way you do with WordPress.

b. Audience - Medium provides bloggers with access to it's audience. Your posts on Medium can get promoted to other viewers on Medium.

c. Ease of Use - Medium is incredibly easy to use. It's easy to make a Medium blog look great because it looks great from the start. Medium does not have much customization ability.

Who Should Use Medium?

Medium is commonly used for long-form storytelling. If you're blogging primarily because you enjoy writing or telling stories, I would recommend blogging on Medium. Medium may not be as effective if you want more design control or are using a blog for marketing purposes.

How to Start Blogging

I talk to people all the time who tell me they know how valuable blogging can be, and they want to start, but they are having trouble getting started. Most people don't know what to write about. Additional reasons include lack of time and difficulty putting thoughts into words. Some people have managed to start a blog, but can't seem to maintain it. The following chapter provides advice on how to kickstart your blogging habit.

1. Start Small

Small habits can lead to bigger habits. Starting with shorter, more frequent blog posts can help you get in to the practice of blogging. Writing a small, even just a 100 word post can help you get over the hardest part of blogging: getting started. From there you can build some momentum to start tackling more ambitious posts. Starting with a long post can be intimidating. Starting small eliminates the barrier to getting started.

2. Set Goals

Setting specific, measurable, and realistic goals can be motivational and force accountability. If you've committed to yourself to write a certain number of blog posts or words within a given period of time, you will feel inclined to do so. I like to set goals on a weekly basis. Reaching the goals can bring confidence, and therefore more motivation.

3. Set a Schedule

Find the time that's best for you to blog. Different people feel more able to focus on writing at different times. Experiment to see which times are most conducive to writing for you. Maybe while you're walking or driving to work you can record yourself talking about a topic that you can later transcribe. I personally like to write on weeknights and weekend afternoons.

4. Talk and Transcribe

Some people find it easier to talk than to write. If that is the case for you, try recording yourself talk about the topic you want to write about. Then transcribe the audio in to blog post format.

5. Brain Dump

Write whatever comes to mind first. There's nothing worse than staring at a blank page and a blinking cursor. Write down the first thoughts on the topic that come to mind. Write an outline and then fill in the blanks. Remove all filters to help you get started.

6. Write Immediately

When you think of an idea for a post, write it immediately. Previously, when I would think of an idea, I would simply make a note of it on my phone or to-do list. This often resulted in forgetting what I actually wanted to write, or simply losing interest in the topic. Now when I think of an idea for a post, I write as much as I can of the post right away. It helps me to write while it's top of mind, and reduces filtering.

7. Conclusion First

Write the conclusion of your blog post first. The conclusion is everything you want the reader to walk away with, in a short and straightforward way. Writing the conclusion first will help you determine what you need to include in the post. Sometimes the conclusion becomes my opening paragraph. Sometimes I break up the sentences in the conclusion across the post. Writing the conclusion first is a quick and easy way to get your main points down and focus the rest of the post.

8. Blog Topics for Beginners

More potential blog topics will be discussed in the next chapter. The next chapter will also address desired outcomes from blogging. The below topics are great for beginning bloggers.

a. Summarize and Expand

Summarize large topics in a short post and then expand from there. For example, to write a post on content marketing, start by writing "content marketing helps attract, engage, and acquire customers." Continue by explaining what attracting, engaging and acquiring are, what specific tactics can be used, some examples of great content marketing, some tips to better engage customers, etc.

b. Curate

Content does not have to be original, unique, or created by you for it to be valuable to your audience. Delivering value to your audience, after all, is the goal of content marketing and blogging. Instead of creating content, another alternative is to curate existing content created by other authors. Write a blog post listing your favorite blog posts on a given topic or write a blog post listing favorite tips and quote the original author.

c. Summarize

Similar to curating, one approach is to summarize news items, articles, research reports, books, or courses. Include your favorite quotes and add commentary. Summarize the key points.

Summarizing a piece of content that's only available in audio or video format could be especially valuable to people who prefer reading to listening. Again, your content does not have to be completely unique, especially when getting started. Topics like this one will help you kick-start your habit and hopefully lead you to writing about more unique or advanced topics later on.

d. Answer a Question You Get Asked

Sometimes it's easier to talk about a topic when you are prompted to do so. Why not answer a basic question, such as "what do you do?," or something more advanced. Answering a more advanced question as a blog post could save you the time of answering it again in the future. Answering a question you get asked frequently can help you organize your thoughts and crystalize your response.

If someone asks a question, it's an indication that they have a need for information on that topic. Therefore, a blog post that answers a question has educational value. Quora may be a good source for questions to address in your blog.

What to Blog About

Before I give you specific topics and ways to generate blog topics, There are two key principles you need to keep in mind:

a. Write about your space, not your product

Remember two things I said previously in this book: first, people don't always search for product names or categories, sometimes they search for information or solutions. Second, write posts that are valuable to your audience to attract them and engage with them. What would you rather click on, "Laundry Detergent: $10", or "How to Clean Grass Stains."

b. Deliver value

Remember, content marketing, including blogs, should deliver entertainment and/or educational value to your audience. Make sure your audience will either learn, be interested, be intrigued, or have fun, when reading your blog post.

Somewhat contrary to the above, the post doesn't have to be directly related to the area of your customers' life that your product or service addresses. It could be valuable to another area of life that your target customer segment is likely to be interested in.

Create a customer persona to determine who exactly your customer is. For example, if you sell expensive art, one customer persona might be people working in finance, in their 30's, living in New York City.

What other than art is someone within that persona likely to get educational or entertainment value from? Perhaps the stock market, personal finance, or golf. A great example of this, is a financial advisor who has a newsletter about golf.

16 Blog Topic Ideas

1. Be a Reporter

Act like a journalist or reporter for a media company that your target audience is likely to read. Write about cool products or companies that might be of interest to your target audience.

Write about a conference or event you attended. Summarize the speakers' talks. Give your opinion on it. This would be especially valuable for people who weren't able to attend the event. If the event was exclusive it will make you look cool. It also shows that you are very involved with the industry.

2. Teach

Write a "how to" or "# tips" post. People love tips and how-to's. They are actionable and the titles illustrate how valuable they may be. In addition, it's often fairly easy to include keyword search terms that you want to rank for in these posts.

To give an oversimplified example, if you're a career coach, a good topic might be "How to Advance Your Career." Someone who needs a career coach is likely to want to read a blog post about how to advance their career.

If you're looking for a job in sales write a post like "How to Prospect a Sales Pipeline" to illustrate to potential employers that you know how to prospect a sales pipeline.

3. One-on-One Interview

There are many benefits to interviewing people, including:

A. If you have a large blog following, you will be helping out the person by promoting his/her business.

B. You don't have to think of the content, just the questions.

C. If you can get a high profile person, it gives the perception that you are well connected.

D. It's a great way to meet people. Reaching out to someone offering press is much more attractive than asking for their time.

E. If you interview someone that's knowledgeable and well spoken, the content can be extremely high quality.

4. Answer Quora Questions

Browse Quora topics that you would like to write about. See what questions are being followed by large numbers of people. If that question was asked and there are a lot of people following it, that's an indication that there is need for information on the topic. Therefore providing that information in the form of a blog post would be of value to your target audience.

If you are a financial advisor, browse the personal finance section. If you see a question such as "What's an IRA?",answer it and then reformat it as a blog post titled "10 Things You Need to Know About IRAs."

5. Do What's Working

Sometimes it's better not to try to reinvent the wheel. If you see a blog post getting a lot of comments and social shares, write something similar, from a different perspective.

6. Ask Your Audience

Blog posts with educational value give the audience knowledge or information that they are seeking. People often seek information on topics where they face challenges. For example, if you need to fix a pipe, you may need to first take some time to learn how to accomplish the repair. A blog post teaching how to fix a pipe could be valuable. "How to Fix a Pipe" could be a great blog post for an ecommerce company that sells hardware to attract customers.

If you are not sure what your audience is having challenges with or needs to learn, ask them.

7. Tweet First

If you have some topics in mind, and you have a large Twitter following, tweet the titles or some of the key points of the blog post before writing it out. See if people engage with the Tweet. If a certain tweet gets more retweets or replies, it could be an indication that people would get more value from a full post on the topic.

8. Hold Office Hours

A great way to learn about what people might want to learn about is to host office hours. Listen for the questions that come up commonly and answer them as blog posts. If you keep getting asked something like "how can I speed up my sales cycles?", write a post such as "4 Ways to Speed Up Your Sales Cycles." You can also use office hours as an opportunity to simply ask people what challenges they face, what they want to learn, and/or what they want you to blog about.

I use a product called SoHelpful to host office hours via phone or video. You can schedule office hours with me at www.sohelpful.me/mikefishbein.

9. Answer Frequently Asked Questions

If you are a content marketing strategist, and a customer asks you "How can I get more customers using content marketing?" Write a post titled "How to get more customers with content marketing." If people often ask you for advice on looking for a job, write your favorite tips as a blog post. If people ask you how to complete a certain task, such as buying a domain name, write a post detailing the process and include screenshots.

10. Write for Different Customers

If your product or service is related to social media marketing, write "social media marketing for startups," "social media marketing for dentists," "social media marketing for job seekers," etc. Adapt the content of the post to the needs of that customer segment.

11. List Resources

Compile a list of the best products, blog posts, YouTube videos, books, etc. relevant to your space. The people whose content you include will probably appreciate it too. They may even share it once you publish it. For example, if your customers are marketers, write a post titled "The 25 Best Link Building Tools."

In addition, comprehensive lists often get linked to, boosting your search ranking. I recently wrote a post titled "The Ultimate List of Customer Development Questions" that was one of my best performing blog posts of all time.

12. Summarize a Book or Research Report

Summarizing is valuable because it saves your audience time. Think of a book your target audience is likely to want to read. Write a post with a title like "# Big Takeaways From X."

13. Give Your Opinion

There's one thing that no one can write better than you: your opinion. If there is breaking news or controversial topic in your space or relevant to your audience, provide your opinion on it. People find it interesting to hear new or unique opinions. Edginess can be entertaining.

14. Re-format Audio or Video Content

Sometimes the hardest part about writing a blog post is just thinking of what to include in the post. To avoid generating a new topic, summarize or transcribe content that you've already produced in audio or video format, or discuss an interview you gave or a presentation at a recent conference.

15. Provide a Free Consultation

If you are a marketing strategy consultant, write about what marketing strategies you would recommend to a given company. Consider writing about a company that you would like to have as a client. Doing so could grab their attention and display your expertise. By providing a free consultation, you are "paying it forward." In addition, you reduce uncertainty your client may have about your ability to help them because you've already begun proving it.

16. Write a Case Study

Consider writing about how a customer used your product to achieve results. Or write a case study about your space in general. For example, if your product is for social media marketers, write a case study about how someone used a certain Twitter strategy to achieve results or on how a given company sourced and hired amazing social media interns.

How to Make Money Blogging

The most common ways to make money blogging are affiliate marketing, displaying advertising, and selling premium content, products, or services. I have made money through affiliate marketing and by selling premium content. This chapter provides a brief summary of how each of these forms of monetization work.

1. Affiliate Marketing

Affiliate marketing is when you sell or market someone else's products and get paid a commission.

Companies with a product to sell are almost always looking for more customers. The companies might start a blog in order to attract more customers. Instead of rebuilding a blog from scratch, or in addition to their own blog, they might contract with affiliate marketers. Affiliate marketers can give a company access to a new, different, or larger audience than what they already have.

There are a few benefits of marketing a company's product as an affiliate, as opposed to working for the company full time. First, you can make your own schedule. You don't need to abide by the company's rules and schedule. Second, you can diversify. You can market multiple products. Diversifying reduces risk because if one product does not sell well you still have others. In addition, if one company fails or goes bankrupt, you still have several other products. If you are working for a company full time that fails, you will need to find a new job.

To make money with affiliate marketing, a large audience on its own will achieve results. You need both 1) a large audience and 2) products that are of interest to your audience.

If you try to market products that your audience doesn't want, they probably won't buy. If you market products that they actually want, there is a much higher likelihood that they will buy.

I am an affiliate marketer of Amazon and Udemy. In both cases, the companies allow me to create unique links to any product that I like. If someone buys a product after clicking through the link, I receive a commission.

One of the largest affiliate networks is CJ Affiliate (http://snip.ly/0up). They provide affiliate markets with a large catalogue of products that they can market to their audience.

2. Advertising

Paid advertising is attractive to marketers because it allows them to attract the attention of their target audience. If their target audience was people who watch a certain TV show or network, they may put a commercial on that TV show or network. If their target audience drives on a certain road, the marketer may place an advertisement on a billboard.

If a marketer's audience reads your blog, they may want to advertise on your blog. The marketer could pay to have some kind of display ad, or other ad unit placed somewhere on your blog.

Most advertisers won't advertise on a blog unless there is a high volume of traffic and the demographics of the traffic are within their target audience. Therefore, it may take a long time before a blog can monetize through advertising.

You can find advertisers for you blog by reaching out to them directly, or by using a product like Google's Adsense. If you would like to target specific companies to advertise on your site, start by analyzing your audience demographics and think about what companies serve those same demographics.

3. Paid Content or Products

Offering paid content, products or services is a great way to monetize a blog. One major benefit it has over advertising is that you can monetize through paid content from day one.

You don't need a large audience in order to offer paid products. One advantage it has over affiliate marketing is that because it's your product and not someone else's, you keep 100% of the revenue.

There are few different types of paid offerings to market through a blog.

a. Ebooks

Write an ebook on the topic of your blog and charge for it. For example, if your blog is about software design, an ebook titled "The Ultimate Guide to Software Design" may be of interest to your target audience.

You can put it behind a paywall, perhaps using a product like Gumroad, and charge as much as you'd like for it. If you've been blogging about software design for a while, you probably already have much of the content you need, so it might not even take you much time.

b. Video Course

Produce a video course on the topic of your blog. If you blog about sales,create a "Sales 101" course. I use a product called Fedora to host and sell my video courses. Fedora makes it easy create a fully functional online school without any technical or design experience. WordPress is to blogs what Fedora is to online schools. There is zero up front cost to use Fedora's basic plan. Check out Fedora at mfishbein.com/fedora.

c. Consulting and Coaching

If you're writing a blog that helps people with a given aspect of their life, offer consulting or coaching services to help them even more. For example, if your blog is about how to market a small business, your audience is likely to be small businesses that are trying to improve their marketing. They may also be interested in speaking with you one on one or having you work actively on their marketing campaigns. Charge a fee for a personal consultation or a monthly retainer to provide continued advice.

d. Self-Publish on Amazon

I continue to be amazed by how easy it is to self-publish a book on Amazon. Self-publishing is radically changing the publishing industry. You know longer have to spend months trying to convince a publisher to publish you. By self-publishing, you also don't have to give up a huge percentage of your sales to a publishers. Amazon takes only a small transaction fee.

Amazon has a massive network of active shoppers. By self-publishing on Amazon, you can reach large new audiences. In addition, many Amazon shoppers have their credit card information stored on Amazon and can complete the checkout process within seconds. The shorter and easier check out process is likely to improve conversion rates as compared to a longer checkout process where shoppers would have to create a new account and/or enter their credit card information.

Not only can self-publishing make you money, it can also be a great way to market your blog or other businesses. Visit kdp.amazon.com to learn more about self-publishing and to start the self-publishing process. You can check out the books I've self-published at mfishbein.com/amazon.

Production

It's very easy to create a book that can be published on Amazon. You do not need any technical abilities. If you already have a blog, you can start by copying and pasting the text you want to include in the book into a Google Document. In order to publish on Amazon, your text document has to be in a certain format. Google Document's format fits the specifications, so you do not need to modify the format of the Google Document.

Editing

You need to modify the content of your book before publishing on Amazon. Amazon screens the web to make sure the contents of the book is not available for free elsewhere. Make sure you change a lot of your blog posts before publishing. If you're charging for your book, you should probably provide a lot more information or value than what you're giving away for free.. It is always effective add more detail or examples.

Marketing

Below are a few ways you can market your book. For more ideas on how you can market a nonfiction book, check out "Growth Hacking with Content Marketing" at mfishbein.com/contentmarketing.

a. Blog - You can market the book by linking to it within your blog posts, on your blog's main page and/or by emailing it to your email subscribers.

b. Reviews - The number and quality of reviews a book has, has a major effect on how a book ranks on Amazon search. It can be quite valuable to rank highly on Amazon's search because many people use Amazon, instead of Google, to search for books and other products.

c. Content Marketing - Try producing content on different platforms and linking back to your book. For example, if your book is about nutrition, start a podcast about nutrition and mention your book in the podcast. Speak at conferences or events focused on health or host a webinar about nutrition. Also consider answering questions on Quora about nutrition and link back to your book. Create YouTube videos about nutrition. And the list goes on.

Paperback

You can create a paperback version of your book at zero upfront cost! A paperback version of your book can be created by using a service called Createspace. Createspace is actually owned by Amazon.

You will need to reformat you Google Document to fit within the guidelines of Createspace's required formatting. It's not very hard to do. You can even have it done for $5 using Fiverr.com. However I recommend doing it yourself though so you have full control over the design.

Book Cover

In order to publish on Amazon or Createspace, you will need to have a book cover. In fact, having a good looking book cover can be extremely important for sales. Amazon and Createspace provide free cover creation tools. However, the covers made using these free tools usually do not come out that great.

If you are a designer, I would recommend putting in some time in effort to make a great looking cover. If you are not a designer, I would recommend hiring a designer. If you do not have a large budget, I would recommend using Fiver.com to have a cover made for just $5. The cover for this book was made on Fiverr.

e. Premium Content

Similar to to offering an ebook, simply make some of your content available to paid subscribers, a newsletter, or simply additional blog posts.

10 Best Tools and Apps for Bloggers

Below are some of the best tools I would recommend bloggers use. Most are free. Some cost a small amount of money or have premium features.

1. Hello Bar

Hello Bar enables you to add a colored bar at the top of your blog with a button that links to your desired page. You can customize the color and text on your Hello Bar.

It's very attention grabbing, so you can use it to drive more traffic to the page of your choosing. For example, use Hello Bar to prompt viewers to sign up for your email list or to send traffic to one of your paid products such as your book on Amazon. You can access Hello Bar at http://snip.ly/u4P.

2. Exit Monitor

Exit Monitor is a lead generation and conversion optimization tool. Exit Monitor tracks the mouse location and velocity of every visitor of a page. It uses that data to detect when a visitor is about to exit your page. Once a potential exit has been detected, Exit Monitor displays a pop up screen offer to the web visitor. This allows for an extra pageview to be displayed for a visitor that would have normally been lost.

You can use the pop up screen to offer something for free in exchange for their email address, a discount coupon, or simply to prompt them to sign up for your email list. You can access Exit Monitor at http://snip.ly/HFO.

3. Mailchimp

Mailchimp is my preferred email marketing solution. It allows you to collect and manage email addresses, send emails, and track results. It easily integrates with WordPress and other blogging platforms and is free to use the basic version.

Mailchimp makes it easy to create well designed emails to send to your email list. It's easy for viewers to sign up for your list and to un-subscribe. Mailchimp also provides analytics on the open and click through rates of your campaigns.

4. Google Analytics

Google Analytics is essential for any online business. It's a product offered by Google that generates detailed statistics about a website's traffic and traffic sources. It also measures and provides analytics on conversions and sales. Using Google Analytics you can gain valuable insights such as how much traffic a given post is generating, how much traffic your site is getting, where your traffic is coming from, and more.

5. Codementor

While most blogging platforms require little or no coding, you may at some point need help doing customizations or integrations. When I need help modifying my WordPress blog or editing the theme in any way, I use Codementor.

Codementor is an online marketplace where you can connect with expert developers via live video calls. You simply enter what you need help with and you get matched with a developer who can help. Sometimes it only takes a few minutes to find some. Many of the developers charge very low hourly rates. I have saved a lot of time and anguish using Codementor. If you use access Codementor through mfishbein.com/codementor, you will get $10 off.

6. Fedora

If you're looking for a way to monetize your blog traffic, Fedora is a great solution. Fedora can provide you with a fully functional online school within hours and at no upfront cost. Using Fedora you can host, and charge for, video courses. You can hose your online school on a custom domain or as a subdomain, such as learn.yourblog.com. Check out Fedora at mfishbein.com/fedora.

7. Buffer

If you're promoting your blog, you're probably using social media. Buffer is an outstanding social media management tool. Buffer's browser plug in enables you to share any page on the web that you're viewing across any or all of your social networks within clicks. It also enable you to schedule your social shares. Buffer is very helpful in ensuring that you are consistently sharing content and helps save a lot of time in doing so.

8. Google Keyword Planner

You need to create a Google Adwords account in order to access Google Keyword Planner, but you do not need to pay for advertising. I use Google Keyword Planner most often to learn about what search terms I should be using in blog posts and titles.

Google Keyword Planner will show you how many searches for given terms occur each month. It will also give you suggestions for other related keywords and phrases that users are searching.

For example, to generate the title of this book, I used this tool to see what kinds of keywords and phrases people were using as it pertains to blogging. I then used those words and phrases in my title, subtitle, and Amazon description. It's important to make sure you're using the words that your customers are using so that they can find you.

9. Sniply

Sniply (http://snip.ly/an4) is a great way to turn your Twitter followers and other connections in to followers of your blog. Sniply allows you to put a "hello bar like" CTA button at the bottom of any page on the web that you share.

If you are sharing someone else's blog post about marketing and your blog is about marketing, use Sniply to display a CTA bar at the bottom of the page linking to your blog. Anyone who clicks on the Sniply link that you share will see this CTA bar and have the option to click to your blog.

Sniply integrates with Buffer, and has a great Chrome plug in, so I'm adding CTAs to pretty much every link I share. Most of the links within this chapter are Snip.ly links. Click any of them to see an example of how to use Sniply.

10. Quora

Quora can be used in a number of different ways by bloggers. Below are my favorite techniques. Most of these are ways to promote your blog. You can view my Quora profile to see exactly how I use Quora at mfishbein.com/quora.

a. Answer Questions

Answering questions that are relevant to your target blog audience is a great way to attract new blog followers. To get the best results from answering questions, provide very thoughtful and detailed answers without being overly promotional. The better your answer is, the more likely it is to get upvoted. The more your answer gets upvoted, the more exposure it gets.

To get traffic from your answers, contextually link to relevant blog posts within the answer. Also suggest they check out other blog posts of yours at the end of the answer. Include a link to your blog in your Quora profile so if anyone clicks on your profile, they can easily find your blog. The name and brief bio of the answer is displayed with every answer. Include the name of your blog or a link to it in your bio.

b. Promote

You can use Quora Credits to promote your answers and blog posts on Quora. Quora credits are awarded when your posts get upvoted, you answer questions that you were asked to answer, when an answer provided by someone you asked to answer gets upvoted, and when questions you ask get followed.

Promotion with Quora Credits works similar to promoted tweets on Twitter. When promoted, the answer will appear in the newsfeed of people who are following the topic.

c. Quora Blog

Create a Quora blog as your primary blog, or to cross-post your blog posts. The benefit of blogging or cross posting is that you can attract a wider audience.

Quora blogs appear in results when people search on Quora, and I've noticed they sometimes rank fairly high in searches in Google. In addition, your blog posts on Quora can get upvoted, which means more exposure and more credits (which can be used to get more exposure).

d. Blog Topic Ideas

If you're ever wondering what to write about, browse questions within the topic of your blog. Many people find it easier to write or talk about something if they are asked a question. Answer questions you see on Quora and then reformat it as a blog post.

In addition, when someone asks a question or follows one, it is of course and indication that they want an answer. Therefore by answering the question, you are delivering value to them. Delivering value is one of the core principles of blogging and content marketing.

e. Learn

Quora is a great way to learn about many different fields. It's often the first place I go to learn about a given topic. There are also some great threads about blogging and marketing on Quora.

If you don't find a question for something you're looking for an answer to, you can post the question yourself. You can then use your Quora credits to ask people who have expertise in the field to answer it.

f. Networking

Quora has a large community of great people. Actively engaging on Quora by commenting on answers and blog posts, following people, direct messaging people, upvoting, etc. is a great way to meet and get to know people.

People on Quora could become friends or colleagues, or may be able to refer you to people who can help you with your blog. Answering questions intelligently can display your expertise to people and help you get found by them.

How to Promote Your Blog

If you're blogging to market a product or service, you will of course need people to read it. If no one sees your blog, it has no value. Building a large audience of engaged blog followers often takes a lot of time. Below are some blog promotion ideas that can help speed up the process.

1. Produce for Different Platforms

Create content in different formats to tap into new networks. Each of the networks described below are like miniature search engines. People go there to search for, browse, and consume content.

Some people are more active on some networks than other networks. So if you were only blogging, you might not be able to reach people that consume mostly video content on YouTube. Below are some of the different platforms you can product content for, and how you can use them to promote your blog.

a. YouTube

YouTube (mfishbein.com/youtube) is the second largest search engine, and the third most visited site globally. People love video! In addition, because Google owns YouTube, YouTube videos tend to rank fairly high in search results.

To get results with YouTube, produce content that's valuable to your target audience. Use the right keywords so they can find it. To get traffic from YouTube to your blog, mention your blog's URL in your video, and include a link to your blog in the video's description.

b. SlideShare

SlideShare is a presentation hosting network. Users can upload PowerPoint, Keynote, PDF or OpenDocument presentations. You can think of SlideShare as "YouTube for presentations." If your blog within categories like Business, technology, health, travel, or education, SlideShare could be a great marketing channel.

To increase the chances of viewers navigating to your blog, make a link to your website accessible to viewers. Include a link in your profile, in your presentation's description and within your presentation. Viewers can click on links within SlideShare presentations. You can access SlideShare at mfishbein.com/slideshare.

c. Udemy

Udemy is an online marketplace for video courses. Anyone can produce a course on any topic and publish it to Udemy. Over 2 million students use Udemy to search for and consume educational content. Courses can be free or paid - you set the price. In addition to it being a great place to learn as a student, and make money as an instructor, it can also be a great marketing channel for bloggers.

Create video courses within field of your blog to attract relevant Udemy students to your course. Mention your blog in all of your lectures and include links to relevant blog posts within the notes for each lecture. You can also make announcements and send promotional emails to your students. Send them relevant blog posts. You can check out Udemy at mfishbein.com/udemy.

d. Podcast

A podcast is an audio broadcast on the Internet. Kind of like a radio show. The Podcast marketplace is like it's own search engine. Podcasts can be subscribed to and downloaded through web syndication or streamed online to a computer or mobile device. Start a Podcast on your niche. Mention relevant blog posts through the show and include links in the show notes. Visit the podcast center in iTunes at snip.ly/0Zr.

e. Quora

Quora (http://mfishbein.com/quora) is a question and answer site with a lot of active viewers. Answer questions that are relevant to and followed by your target audience. Provide strong, detailed answers that provide value to your target audience. Link to your blog in your Quora profile, in your bio line for the answer, and within the answer if appropriate.

f. Amazon

Amazon has a massive network of users that search Amazon for products. By self-publishing a book on Amazon you can tap into a proverbial fire house of traffic. The book can be as short as long as you'd like and you can set the price as you'd like. Self-publish a book on the topic of your blog. Link to blog posts and your primary blog domain within the book.

2. Social Media

a. Twitter

Share

My typical tweet structure when sharing is a blog post is "[post title] [link] [relevant hashtags]." For example, "How to Use a Blog to Market Your Business http://qr.ae/thBLo #blogging #contentmarketing"

Do some searching on Twitter to determine which hashtags to use. Some hashtags have active conversation and many people following or engaging.

If you mentioned anybody in the blog, or if there is anybody in particular you think would benefit from reading the post, mention them in the Tweet by including their @handle. By mentioning them, they may be more likely to respond or retweet, giving you more exposure.

Find People Expressing a Need

Use Twitter's search functionality to find people using keywords relevant to your blog. Engage with people who fit your target demographic. When appropriate, reply to their tweets with blog posts that might be helpful.

For example, if someone tweets that their building a landing page, reply with a blog post your wrote on landing page design. There are a few great apps you can use to search Twitter for relevant conversations quickly and easily. Check out "13 Twitter Apps: Automate and Optimize Your Twitter Marketing" at mfishbein.com/twitterapps.

b. LinkedIn

There are great two ways to get more views from LinkedIn: status updates and groups.

Status updates will be seen by your connections and the connections of anyone who "likes" your update.

Groups are great regardless of how many connections you have. Search for groups related to your industry, your target audience, or the topic of your blog post. Join them. Share your posts in those groups. Add some personalized commentary.

c. Google+

Share your posts as a status updates. People who have you in their circles will see them.

Post to communities. Start by finding relevant communities (similar to LinkedIn, above). You can post directly to communities from the share container on your home screen.

You can add hashtags to your status according to the topic of the blog to increase the chances of someone finding it when searching.

Also...and this is a big one...per Moz's Search Ranking Factors, the number of Google +1's a page has is the second most influential factor for how it will rank on search engines!

d. Facebook

Share your posts on your personal profile or business page. Posts that have a picture will stand out a lot more.

Also check out Facebook groups that pertain to the interests of your audience. For example, if I were to distribute a blog post about promoting a blog post, I would think about who would want to get views on their blog posts.

Who uses blog posts to promote their product/service? Many do, but I would focus on some the Facebook groups I'm most interested in and already a part of --

i.e. authors/book marketers, Udemy instructors/course marketers, etc.

3. Niche Social Networks

Who is your target customer segment? Who are you trying to reach? Where do they hang out? Go where your customers go.

For example, photographers might be hanging out on Instagram. Business people who do a lot of networking might be on LinkedIn, oHours, etc.

People looking to rent an apartment hang out on AirBnb and Craigslist. Developers hang out on StackOverflow and GitHub.

Many industries and interest groups have online forums or discussion boards. Think about what social networks your target audience is likely to be active on, especially the networks that pertain to your product area.

4. Content Distribution Networks

Reddit is a "social news" site where registered users can submit links and users promote the articles they like. The most voted articles get promoted on the front page of Reddit, which can lead to massive exposure.

There are a few other article distribution/link sharing networks that I use that pertain to startups: Hacker News, Quibb, and Growth Hackers. There are probably others for different industries that you'll want to search for.

Try asking friends, colleagues, or family to upvote your posts on these sites to get more exposure.

5. Direct

While sending specific people blog posts one by one may not be a scalable traffic acquisition strategy, it can have big payoffs over time, and is often needed when first starting.

Sending blog posts to people directly can ensure that your target audience sees it, as well as enable you to reach out to influential people by offering them something instead of asking for their time. Below are a few types of people who may benefit from your blog posts:

a. Audience

Email your blog posts directly to your target audience. If you blogging about product management, so you can get a job in product management at a startup, email a blog post you wrote on product management to a startup founder who it would be valuable to. You're not being annoying if the post is truly valuable.

b. Influencers

Email your blog posts directly to influential people who could help share your blog. For example, I wrote a blog post about the higher education bubble and sent it to a popular economist who hosts a radio show/podcast and often speaks on CNBC. He then shared it on Twitter to all of his followers.

c. Curators

Email your blog posts directly to people who curate content and share it with their audience. Some bloggers have "best resources" pages or blog posts for given topics. Reach out to these people and suggest they take a look at your post on the topic.

For many industries and topics, there are email newsletters that send out the best relevant articles on a weekly, daily, or monthly basis. In the startup world, some of the popular article curating newsletters are Mattermak and Startup Digest.

6. Guest Blogging

Guest blogging is when you write a blog post and have it published by another blogger. Some blogs accept guest posts, others do not. Most blogs will restrict you from publishing your guest post on other blogs, including your own.

Most blogs will permit you to include a link to your blog in your "profile" for the blog post, or to link to other relevant blog posts within the guest blog post. Guest blogging can help you in two ways:

   A.   Audience - When your article is published on someone else's blog, that blog's audience sees it.

   B.   SEO - Having your domain linked to by another domain (link building), improves search ranking on Google.

7. Search Engine Optimization

Many, many people go to Google to find stuff, blog posts included. Social networks, such as Twitter, are more for "passive consumption." You see what articles come your way and click on the ones you want to check out. When there's something more specific that people are looking for, they go to Google.

Therefore, you want to improve your search ranking as much as you can so your posts will surface higher than your competitors. This book contains an entire chapter on search engine optimization. Read that chapter to learn more about how SEO works and how you can use it to promote your blog.

8. Blog Commenting

Search for blogs and blog posts related to your blog and blog posts. Write value added comments on the blog posts you find. For example, if you wrote a post titled "7 Best Apps for Social Media Marketers," search for blogs and blog posts about social media marketing strategy. Add tips or your opinion about the blog posts you find and then offer your blog post on 7 apps to help the author and the readers with what was recommended in the blog post.

After I wrote a blog post about startup studios, a rather niche topic, searched Google for "startup studio." I found a few blog posts about startup studios. I then provided personalized commentary on each blog post and pasted a link to my blog post, offering it if anyone wanted hear more about my thoughts on the topic.

9. Email List

By allowing people to opt in to receiving your blog posts by email, you increase your potential to get traffic on your posts. Every time you publish a post you will have a list of people to email. Mailchimp or Aweber are some of the most popular email marketing products. I use Mailchimp.

How to Build an Email List

Below are a few tips for getting more people to sign up for your email list:

i. Display your email opt in form prominently on your blog.

ii. Display your email opt in form at the end of each blog post.

iii. At the end of a blog post write, "To learn more about this topic, sign up for my email newsletter", and link to your optin form.

iv. Offer something in exchange for signing up, such as an ebook.

10. Networking

Networking can help your blog in several ways. Below are some of the biggest.

i. Social Media - More connections on LinkedIn, Twitter, Facebook and Google Plus means more people will see the blog posts you share there.

ii. Referrals - Your network may be able to introduce you to journalists or other bloggers for press or guest blogging opportunities.

iii. Shares - Having a strong network of folks that like you and want to help you may lead to more social shares. Your network can share your content on their social channels and promote your to their audiences.

To learn more about building a professional network, check out "How to Build an Awesome Professional Network" at mfishbein.com/network.

How to Write a Blog Post: 9 Tips

Everyone has their own style for writing blog posts. Different readers have different preferences. How you write your blog posts will likely depend on the topic of your blog. For example, a blog post about learning software development would likely be very detailed and dry instructional guides, where as a blog about dating would likely be very personal and emotional.

Below are some of my favorite tips writing blog posts. You might want to apply some, none, or all of these to your writing. Use your judgment based on the topic of your blog to decide which tips could be effective for your blog.

1. Goldilox Length

Write posts that are long enough to deliver value and have character, but not so long that it's intimidating or overly time consuming to read. Get to the point, and don't include too much fluff, but make sure you're adding enough character and detail. I usually aim for about 700-1200 words. Sometimes I go under, sometimes I go over.

2. Catchy Title

The title is often the first thing a reader will see when deciding to read the post. It could be via Tweet, email, Facebook, or otherwise. If the title is interesting and attention grabbing it is more likely to get clicked than one that is dry.

Use a unique title that clearly explains what the blog post is about and what value the reader will get from reading it. For example, if you have a blog post about content marketing, don't title it "Content Marketing." Instead, title it something like "How Content Marketing Can Get Your More Fans, Followers, and Customers." Titles that start with "how to" or "# tips" are very popular.

3. Deliver Value

As discussed throughout this book, blog posts, and all forms of content marketing, should deliver educational or entertainment value. The more value your readers get, the more likely they are to return for more, engage with you further or potentially buy your product, or share it with their friends.

4. Show Character

Be authentic. Share your unique opinions. Tell stories and share your own experiences. Don't be afraid to use slang, jargon, or less than perfect grammar if it adds the right character. I regularly use ellipses and emoticons in my blog posts and email newsletters.

5. Use the Right Keywords

Use Google Keyword Planner and other keyword research tools to determine which keywords and phrases you should be using in your title and body. Using keywords and phrases relevant to how people are searching and improve your search ranking.

You would be surprised that the words you use are not always the words people use when they search on Google. For example, "business ideas" is a much more popular search term than "startup ideas."

6. Strong First Sentence

The first line can make or break a blog post. If it's great, readers will be intrigued to keep reading. If it's boring, they may lose interest and browse away.

7. Clear Conclusion

I sometimes include a bullet pointed list of the key takeaways from the post. It allows readers to get value from the post quickly and easily.   A short paragraph with some closing remarks may also be helpful.

8. Include Sub Headings

Including sub headings within a blog post help to make it more readable and organized. Break up your blog post with a different sub heading to highlight and separate the main points or topics of the post. For example, in this chapter, I've added a subheading for each tip.

9. Goldilox Frequency

You don't want your readers to forget about you, but you don't want them to get sick of you either. You want to indulge your readers, but also keep them craving more.

I try to blog about once per week. You may want adjust your frequency depending on how long your posts are. If you are writing "epic" posts that are very long. Less than once a week may be fine. If you are writing short posts of just a few hundred words, more frequently may more effective.

As your community grows larger and more engaged, they may want more frequent content. If your have an email list, you might not want to email them more than a couple times per week, as they could get irritated by receiving too many emails.

Search Engine Optimization 101

Search engine optimization (SEO) is very important for bloggers and internet markers. It is also a very complex topic. This chapter will cover some of the most essential information about SEO and provide you some of the most high impact advice.

How Search Works

Understanding what Google's "job" is helps inform how to improve content to boost search engine ranking. Google's job is to give searchers the most relevant and high quality search results.

People search Google to get the best possible results. To improve it's ability to return the most relevant and valuable information possible, Google needs to rank the massive amounts of content on the web.

There is so much content on the web, that Google could not possibly manually screen every site and rank it. So it uses an algorithm to do it automatically. It's not always perfect, but given Google is the largest search engine and the number one visited site on the web, people seem generally happy with the results they get when searching.

How does Google determine what the most valuable and relevant content is? What would indicate that a given piece of content is high quality and relevant? Many things...such as:

I.   Matching keywords / Relevance
II.   "Endorsements" / Links / Social media activity
III. Popularity / Authority

To improve a website's ranking, a marketer can make some optimizations to tell Google that it's site is the best result for the searcher. Below are some tactics you can use to boost your search ranking.

7 Easy and High Impact Ways to Boost Search Ranking

1. Boost Authority

Search engines typically correlate value and popularity. The more popular a page or domain, the more valuable the information contained therein must be. Makes sense right? Think of a page view as a "vote." If someone views a page it must be a sign that there is something of value there.

Authority has two categories: page authority and domain authority. Page authority pertains to a given page, such as a blog post. Domain authority refers to the site overall.

To boost your site's authority, get more views, Google Plus "+1s", Facebook likes, comments, and shares.

2. Build Links

Google believes that if a site or page has been linked to by another site or page, that it must be high quality. Think about it in real world terms...if a well respected politician endorses a certain candidate, people often perceive that candidate as being strong. If a friend recommends their dentist to you, you would probably believe the dentist is good.

Links are like endorsements of the web. When someone writes a blog post and links to another site for a certain topic, it's an indication that the linked to site is of value.

How to Build Links

i. Guest posting is a great way to build links. Reach out to blogs in your space and offer to write a guest post. Link back to your domain or a page (i.e. blog post) contextually within the post, and/or in your bio section of the blog.

ii. Press is another good, though more challenging, way to get linked to. If you are a startup or have accomplished something big, some blogs might be interested in writing you about you. Most media companies have an email address or form for submitting news.

iii. Write amazing blog posts, and reach out to people who curate content. Some bloggers and websites have "resources" pages. Others create "round ups" of the best articles of the day or week.

After I wrote a post called "The Ultimate List of Customer Development Questions," I searched google for "startup resources" and "startup roundup." If my post was relevant to their blog and audience, I reached out to them suggesting they might be interested in including it. I got a few high quality backlinks as a result.

3. Research Keywords

Text relevancy is another factor used to determine what results to show to a searcher. For example, if you search for "sports scores," a blog post titled "sports scores" is probably going to be closer to what you want than one title "zoo hours."

Do some keyword research to determine what people are searching for as it pertains to your niche. Google Keyword Planner is a great free tool for doing keyword research. Here are some things to look for when evaluating keywords:

a. Searches

If a large number of people are searching a given keyword, that's an indication there is demand for relevant sites. Google Keyword Planner measures and displays this as "Avg. monthly searches."

b. Intent

Does the keyword indicate buying intention? For example, "buy [product]", "hire a [profession]" or "[product] [size/specification]" is probably more likely to be from someone with the intent to buy.

A search like "[product]" is probably from someone who is more in the research or casual browsing phase. "How to [activity]" shows more intent to learn how to do that activity than "[activity]." So if you're selling a book, or course, that could be a great term to target.

c. Competition

Little or no competition can actually be a bad sign. It probably means that there's little money to be made in those keywords. Or else another marketer would probably be targeting them.

Too much competition means it may be harder for you to rank for those terms.

Google Keyword Planner displays the relative competitiveness of the term in the "competition" column. In addition, the "suggested bid" column shows how much people are willing to pay for those clicks. It's likely the more someone is willing the pay the more they're making back in return.

Do some qualitative research to see how strong your competition is. For example, if you search the keyword and multiple big name blogs come up, such as the New York Times, etc., it may be hard to compete with them.

Conversely, if your search returns some small niche blogs, you may have a chance at achieving a higher ranking than them. You can also go to ecommerce sites like Amazon to see what's selling.

4. Keyword Optimize

Use relevant, high volume, low competition keywords in your headlines, meta descriptions, title, etc., to optimize your site. When getting linked to from another site, use the relevant keyword as the anchor text. Pick a domain that matches your keyword if possible.

5. Pick a Good Domain Name

A site's actual domain name also has an effect on search rankings. Having an exact match, .com domain name will provide a boost. For example, "turkeytrees.com" will rank higher than "bushchicken.com" when someone searches "turkey trees", all else being equal.

.com, .net, and .org domains rank higher than other domain endings. Country relevant domain endings, such as .us, will rank higher for searches made in that given country.

Domains with numbers are penalized. Longer domains also rank lower than shorter domains.

6. Blog on WordPress

Wordpress is a blogging platform that makes it really easy to improve SEO. It's easy to edit link structures, meta descriptions etc. Yoast, and other WordPress plugins make it easier to improve SEO.

7. Google Plus +1s

According to Moz, a page's number of Google +1s is more highly correlated with search rankings than any other factor. In addition, links to posts are followed, meaning they pass link equity on as well. So posting on Google Plus is similar to link building.

Google Plus is a network that marketers need to use! Build a network on Google Plus and share your blog posts there.

Blogging for Business Networking

Amazingly, blogging can actually help you with professional networking. Blogging can help you accomplish several core networking strategies.

Blogging is a great way to engage your existing contacts, as well as reach a new audience. Below are six core networking strategies and how blogging can help us accomplish each of them. If you would like to learn more about business networking, check out "How to Build an Awesome Professional Network" by visiting mfishbein.com/network.

1. Offer Value

One of the core principles of effective business networking is to first make the effort to be helpful and add value to people before expecting anything in return. When your network gets stronger, you get stronger. Blogging is a great way to deliver valuable content to your network.

Writing content that's of interest to your audience, such as "how-tos" or summarizing research you've conducted, is a great way to be helpful. For example, if you're an expert in sales, share your knowledge of various sales tactics. If you're an expert in the healthcare industry, research you've conducted on the industry may also be of interest.

2. Build Your Reputation

People like to have professional relationships with others they respect, admire, and/or see as potentially being valuable to their career or business. Blogging is a great way to display your expertise. Write about topics to impress your network in a non-imposing way. Writing your perspectives and providing analysis and opinion will help you to be recognized as an expert.

Write about your recent learnings and accomplishments. When people understand the value that you have, they be more inclined to stay in touch with you or connect you to others in their network.

3. Be Authentic

While there's no perfect substitute for in-person interaction, blogging is a great way to build rapport with people. When you write in an authentic voice, your character shines through.

Blogging can provide a great supplement for people to get to know you better and build rapport. Tell stories and share your opinion to show your character and help people get to know you.

4. Cast a Wide Net

People are often inclined to share great content with their peers and via their social channels. By reaching a wide audience, you increase the chances of people reaching out to you directly. The audience you reach with your blog could turn into strong professional relationships.

In-person events and meetings can be time consuming; blogging allows you to network in a more time-effective way. In addition, when you're reaching out to or meeting new people, if someone has read your posts, they may feel more inclined to respond and meet with you. To increase your visibility, simply write awesome content that people enjoy and get value from.

5. Stay in Touch

Sharing blog posts on social networks such as LinkedIn, Facebook, and Twitter, is a great way to stay on top of the mind of your connections. Everyone's busy, and many busy people know a lot of people. If you don't stay in touch with busy people, it can be easy for them to forget about you.

Simply seeing your blog post on their LinkedIn feed can be enough for you to stay in touch with people. It's also much less time consuming than meeting everyone you know for coffee once a week, or even sending them emails.

6. Promote Your Network

Promoting people in your network is a great way to be helpful. If a contact has big news, cover it on your blog. An interview with the person may also be of value to your audience.

Offering your network a guest post on your blog would be especially helpful if your audience is large and relevant to your contact. Linking back to a contact's blog or website when contextual to a post you're publishing is a small but very nice way to promote your network. When your network gets stronger, you get stronger.

Key Takeaways

Writing content that's valuable to your audience and displays your expertise is an effective way to build your professional network. Blogging is a great way to stay in touch, update, and build rapport with your network. If you would like to learn more about business networking, check out "How to Build an Awesome Professional Network" by visiting http://mfishbein.com/network.

Conclusion

Blogging is an amazing way to market a business, organize your thoughts, reach an audience, meet new people, and potentially make money.

For an entrepreneur, startup, or consultant, blogging is a great way to attract, engage, and acquire customers. Write blog posts that have educational or entertainment value.

The hardest part about blogging is getting started. The next hardest part is building a large audience. However you do not need a large audience in order to get value from blogging.

To build a bigger audience, promote your blog post by sharing it with them on the networks your target audience spends time on, building an email list, guest blogging, and sending it to influencers directly.

The most common ways to make money blogging are through affiliate marketing, advertising, and offering paid products, content, or services.

Blogging has been an incredibly fun and valuable experience for me. I have benefited personally, professionally, and financially. I hope that this book can help you do the same.

What's Next?

If you enjoyed the book, please leave a review on Amazon by visiting mfishbein.com/amazon.

Connect with me on Twitter at twitter.com/mfishbein. I use Twitter to stay in touch with my professional network and reach new audiences. I share a lot of articles related to startups on Twitter.

Check out my personal blog at mfishbein.com. On my personal blog I write mostly about startups, marketing, and my experiences as an entrepreneur in New York City.

Additional Resources

To learn more about content marketing, check out my book "Growth Hacking with Content Marketing" at http://mfishbein.com/contentmarketing. This book provides a lot more ideas for using content marketing to increase website traffic and grow a business.

To learn more about business networking, check out my book "How to Build an Awesome Professional Network" at http://mfishbein.com/network. This book teaches you strategies and tactics for meeting and building relationships.

To learn more about business ideas, product development, and how to figure out what your audience wants, check out my book "Customer Development for Entrepreneurs" at http://mfishbein.com/custdev. This book is like a tactical guide to "Lean Startup" metholody.

Enroll in Startup College at stpcollege.com for courses on automating twitter marketing, content marketing, and more. Startup College is an online school for enterpreneurs, small businesses, and startups. As a thank you for reading this book, you can apply the discount code "SL" to get 30% off of any course!